HOW TO KNOW…

THAT YOU KNOW…

THAT YOU ARE SAVED…

Shirley Ann Young

COPYRIGHT ©2017 by Shirley Ann Young
All rights reserved.
Printed in the United States of America
ISBN 978-0-692-88201-6

CONTENTS

CAPTION

CHAPTER 1: TRUTH	3
CHAPTER 2: DESTINY/DESTINATION	5
CHAPTER 3: FREEDOM	7
CHAPTER 4: ENDURETH	10
CHAPTER 5: FAITH	13
CHAPTER 6: EXAMINE	15
CHAPTER 7: ETERNITY	16
CHAPTER 8: WILLINGNESS	17
CHAPTER 9: SIN-NATURE	19
CHAPTER 10: SEEDETH	22
CHAPTER 11: INTROSPECTION	25
CHAPTER 12: SELF-PITY	28
CHAPTER 13: TRUE/WORSHIP	30
CHAPTER 14: BELIEVERS	34
CHAPTER 15: FEARLESS	37
CHAPTER 16: FERVENTLY	39
CHAPTER 17: GRACE	41
CHAPTER 18: CHANGE	43

POEM---'MY-MY'

DEDICATION:

{IN HONOR OF THE FATHER, THE SON, AND THE HOLY SPIRIT}

"ALL IN ALL"

CAPTION

Approximately in my early 20s, I acknowledged that the Lord saved me when I repented of my sins as I walked to the altar at my home church as I listened to the precious Holy Spirit.

But little did I know that there was more to this walk of faith as even clueless in that I would be gripped by lukewarmness.

Especially, for years I lived by the notion of the ½ truth that the Lord loved me no matter what and surely to know I was not so bad after all.

To be clear, the truth is that the Lord loves all of us unconditionally; however, the ½ truth relates to the excuse which states 'not that bad after all' to downplay the root of one's sin-nature which limits the ability of true change.

Although I prayed often, I still had no freedom in thinking 'not that bad after all' because it did not appease the guilt that I felt when I sinned. But now I know the awesome embrace of being born again captivated by repentance with the unquenchable desire to live holy know matter the costs.

WELL,

This validation did not come until my early 30s. At that time, as I was earnestly seeking the Lord, a strong sense of conviction came on me while I was at work one day and I said, 'if it cost me everything I will follow thee.' As soon as these words were spoken out of my mouth, I felt this boundlessness freedom by the Holy Spirit from the embodiment of my walk to the alter to presently 34 years of age which astonished my desire even more to share Jesus.

AND EVERYTHING SEEMED GOOD.

But little did I know that at the age of 37, my life would come to a crashing halt of a 4 to 9 month trial. Why me? Of lowliness, I begin to doubt what it even meant to be SAVED.

I became so frantic because I could not hear the Lord's voice. Oh, what a terrible feeling when you know the sheer embrace of the Lord and you can no longer hear. At this point, I wallowed in self-pity.

SOMEHOW,

With a little faith, I managed to seek the Lord as more intensely and the Holy Spirit told me about the backwardness of my lukewarm state.

Primarily, I was blinded by shallow repentance which enabled the devil to tempt me with the same lie but a different tactic especially in my career as uprooted the manifestations of sin: such as fear to cowardliness of what others expected of me rather than being totally depended on the Lord. The stain of unbelief came when I doubted the Lord on rather or not he could help me in the circumstance because I was blinded by worldly success and the predominate root to conclude I was my own worst enemy because I was steep in lukewarmness as underscored by insecurity.

CHAPTER 1: TRUTH

True....

We, as the Body of Christ, have heard that we are no longer under the law which is true. Of that being said, one must take in account the deeper root of what this means. Emotionally, our flesh-man cannot keep the law because we will pick and choose what we consider to be holy, or dismiss the **Word** altogether as we may consider it too hard when we are driven by our-own selfish desires.

And I know all too well, the snare of fleshliness or emotionalism which lead to unholy decisions in congruent to spiritual numbness which seems like a overtone to my life's challenges.

However, I thank the Lord for his saving grace for the truth of being born again to acknowledge that the flesh does not have domain when we inhabit the truth of the inceptive victory of Jesus Christ's death and resurrection which enables one's free will to walk uprightly through maturity and confessions.

17 *"Therefore if any man be in Christ, he is a new creature: old things are passed away; behold all things are become new." (2 Corinthians 5:17).*

Personally, this newness is a continuous process as we adhere to the Lord's will and the need to be cleanse. In that, one must exemplify not to walk according to the flesh.

****

Apostle Paul was inclined by the Lord to say, 19 " Now, the works of the flesh are manifest, which are these; Adultery, fornication, uncleanness, lasciviousness, 20 Idolatry, witchcraft, hatred, variance, emulations, wrath, strife, seditions, heresies, 21 Envying, murders, drunkenness, retellings, and such like: of…which I tell you before, as I have also told you in time past, that they which do such things shall not inherit the kingdom of God." (Galatians 5: 19-21).

As such (Luke 3:8) "bring forth therefore fruits worthy of repentance," to be strengthen by the Holy Ghost, Our Helper, & the Revealer of all Truth.

Definitely, I am more aware that my new life in Christ is set on eternity when I choose to listen & adhere to the guidance of the Holy Spirit. 22 …. "The fruit of the Spirit is love, joy, peace, longsuffering, gentleness, goodness, faith. 23 Meekness, temperance: against such there is no law". (Galatians 5: 22-23).

To correspond, I & we as children of God must grasp the choice to shun evil of the determinate to be holy.

Chapter 2: Destiny/Destination

It is our destiny to know that we have been birthed in an everlasting Kingdom!

>>>The Kingdom Within>>>

The Pharisees asked Jesus,….20 when the kingdom of God should come, he answered them and said 20The kingdom of God cometh not with observation: 21 Neither shall they say, Lo here! Or, lo there! for, behold, the kingdom of God is within you. (Luke 17:20-21).

In that, I am reminded of the new Birth as related to Nicodemas when Jesus said, 5 … Verily, verily, I say unto thee, except a man be born of water and of the Spirit, he cannot enter into the kingdom of God. (John 3:5).

Also, John the Baptist foretold beforehand, 11 "I indeed baptize you with water unto repentance: but he that cometh after me is mightier than I, whose shoes I am not worthy to bear; he shall baptize you with the Holy Ghost, and with fire:" (Matthew 3:11).

And to live this truth-Apostle Paul said, 20 "I am crucified with Christ: nevertheless I live; yet not I, but Christ liveth in me: and the life which I now live in the flesh, I live by the faith of the Son of God, who loved me, and gave himself for me." (Galatians 2:20).

And with this commitment to the Lord Jesus Christ, I know that I am set apart even for an EXCEPTIONAL cause, THE GREAT COMMISSISON to bring others into the Kingdom in which being a willing vessel to allow the Holy Spirit to work mightily within me.

Additionally, our destiny is complete through Jesus Christ as we as believers live unto the new Birth which assures even our destination: Jesus said, 1 Let not your heart be troubled: ye believe in God, believe also in me. 2 In my Father's house are many mansions: if it were not so, I would have told you. I go to prepare a place for you. 3 And if I go and prepare a place for you. I will come again, and receive you unto myself; that where I am, there ye may be also. 4And whither I go ye know, and the way ye know. (John 14:1-4).

CHAPTER 3: Freedom

When we accept Jesus as our Lord and Savior, freedom is inevitable. But we can only feel SECURE with the indwelling of the Holy Spirit as the prominent account of the disciples when they were in the upper room in Jerusalem:

Acts 2:1-4

1 "And when the day of Pentecost was fully come, they were all with one accord in one place. 2 And suddenly there came a sound from heaven as of a rushing mighty wind, and it filled all the house where they were sitting. 3 And there appeared unto them cloven tongues like as of fire, and it sat upon each of them. 4 And they were all filled with the Holy Ghost, and began to speak with other tongues, as the Spirit gave them utterance."

So, as the Body of Christ, our Pentecost experience may differ from the passage above; but it is prominent to happen.

As for me, the Holy Spirit came in the fullness that I ever known his presence thereof with my desperation to be upright before the Lord; so-I said in my 30s, "If it cost me everything Jesus, I will follow thee." And at that moment, I felt 'unspeakable' joy and peace. This is when I realized I was on one accord with the Lord because with deep adoration I only thought about pleasing him. And this is the day that I acknowledged the Lord in such a way not my will but HIS will be done.

****

So, again, this fullness happened when I had to make a choice of the mix of career status. This wave of catalyst thinking came around the times when I was earnestly seeking the Lord by meditating on the Word, having a bountiful pray life, and with regular fasting that I heard an unknown language in my ears as I awoke one morning. I quickly shared what I heard with my husband. Until this day, I am still delighted by this moment.

This brings me to the account that the Lord has always been with me as truth of the Holy Spirit even before a sound of **'DIDIOSHA'DIDIOSHA'** in my ears which is interpreted **"Praise be the Lord,"** or the alter call experience of all I can remember it had to be sometime after my first born son between the age of 16-20s, and the base of knowing about the Lord at an early age as my mom taught me God is **real**.

I even remember in grade school going to music class and just to think that we thought that we only changed classes when we got to junior high. But anyway to get back to music class, I remember that the music teacher taught the class this song, 'He got the whole world in his hands.' Amazingly, I enjoyed singing this song; especially admiring the big poster in the room as I sang. The poster had the globe of the world as it was held up by the character of God' hands, and I thought that this was something!

In my teen years with the dynamic of going to church, I adopted the 1/2 truth scenario...not that bad after all: however, now I know better of compassion to exclaim I love the Lord to a stance of obedience to even accept correction. Jesus said, 15 If ye love me, keep my commandments. (John 14:15). When we seek God and desire obedience, it is AMAZING because even in this---- the Lord still takes the lead per clarification of my heart desire to say, I love you, Lord!

So, to be clear, the Holy Spirit speaks to us all; however, to be filled with the Holy Spirit and to operate in the giftings thereof, we must have an instantaneous desire to obey the Lord at all costs.

What costs?

First of all, the cost that became most evident in my life assigns to the systematic rejection by others. You know--- people that consider you strange when you want conform to worldliness and others who think that you are a **Know- it- all**. But of a truce, I must also take responsibility that my insecure moments caused people to have a limited impression about me. And last but not least, the battle that satan brings against us as believers is more intense; especially, things happening back to back to the excursion of weakness.

Consequently, the supreme cost that seemed to be farthest from my mind is rather or not I am willing to give up my sense of security to the complexity of trials/tribulations even to persecution. So, this perpetuates the question: Will I remain willing to follow the Lord at all cost?

Now, as believers, we are not perfect. (TRUE). However, the sacrifice that Jesus endured on the cross did not only save us unto him, but also gave us the freedom to overcome any temptation or entrapment.

CHAPTER 4: ENDURETH

According to the American Heritage Dictionary, Endure means to carry on through, despite hardships; undergo; to continue in existence; last; to suffer patiently without yielding.

To make it known, my walk with the Lord has not been easy. In 2015 to specify again, I went through the hardest six to nine month trial of my life. I could not understand why I became so shaken by the devastating pitfalls of depression and anxiety. In that, some of you may be reading this and asking yourself, 'Don't we all go through bumps in the road of emotional insecurity.' However, I came to the realization that this ordeal was much more than typical SADDNESS.

Why me?

Before things begin to unravel in my life, I went through a period in which I FELT everything was good: My husband has always adored me, I had reached a sense of heighten self-esteem; as a mother I was more connected with my children; and not to mention my career was at a phase of the upmost accomplishment.. Then, this blanket of goodness was shattered by unexpected thoughts of fear & guilt.

Unfortunate, the pressure that I felt seemed only confined to my career as something unforeseen was happening which caused instability of which intensified the elephant in the room.

And to be truthful now, I did understand why my situation was chaotic. I was in denial about this shakiness which caused my brokenness.

You see when I said that if "it cost me everything"…, this notion became the forefront in which I said I would no longer compromise to meet the unwarranted demands of my career.

When I started working at my own pace as efficient as I could, I was cheerful and excited to have my job all mapped out. Eventually, my heightened security was shattered by one meeting in which upper management said that whatever it takes I must be more progressive in quota. And I would be the first to admit my skill set still could have been better as instability of worth. To associate, this business meeting was the trigger in which I was gradually no longer in tune with the commitment of integrity, I started back willfully sinning as uncured by the bounds of deception.

As long as I was in denial, this became a playground for the enemy to interrupt my life in which I had to deal with heightened circumstances more pervasive than a normal workday---schemes on every side of spiritual warfare. I was bombarded my negative thoughts I even saw the enemy dynamics of working through people around me.

This was no longer just a battle to keep my job but spiritually to keep my sanity. In retrospect, I chose my sanity over my career as I gave my 30-day notice.

Why?

I was still baffled about **why** I didn't stand to overcome compromise to the overtone of weakness.

Of reflection, this situation was not just about a weaken or fallen state; however, as I confided in my best friend / Sister-in-Christ, she encouraged me to understand that the Lord wanted me to see that I made a commitment to Him. *'if it cost me everything that I will follow'*

So, in retrospect, I allowed my job to become that care of deviation as now I know better as words that were inspired by the Bishop.

Confession that I am doing better

Therefore, my career itself was not the declarative root of the problem; however, it was my perception to know that God's standard upholds over man's ways.

IT'S PERSONAL!

So, just to clear, I truly admire all the wonderful and hardworking people that I came to know in the profession in which their story is not like mine and that we are called to a line of service in which we can grow in every arena of our lives...

At this point, I am thankful that the Lord gave me enough strength to cry out through clarity of walking, praying, and reading my Bible. And the Lord spoke to me about this **CROSSROAD** in my life.

The Lord Jesus said, Shirley, "You are lukewarm."
Tearfully, I knew the Lord was right, because I compromised my faith many times by excusing myself to do wrong in satisfying my own heart's desires.

DISCLOSURE TO CHANGE!

My Lord, My Lord, Help Me to Turn & Endure?

CHAPTER 5: FAITH

In such, I did minimized my faith to only the connection of endurance & even to just how the Lord could bless me.

But now I am more in tune with where the premise of our faith should also align to declare that Jesus is coming again. And until he comes, I and we, as the Body of Christ, must walk according to the Spirit of God.

5 Jesus said, I am the vine, ye are the branches: He that abideth in me, and I in him, the same bringeth forth much fruit: for without me ye can do nothing. (John 15:5).

Even to operate in this truth of faith, we must exhibit the unconditional love of God, which is the greatest gift of similitude, charity.

What is Love==**CHARITY**? 4 "Charity suffered long, and is kind: charity envieth not; charity vaunteth not itself, is not puffed up, 5 Doth not behave itself unseemly, seeketh not her own, is not easily provoked, thinketh no evil; 6 Rejoiceth not in iniquity, but rejoiceth in the truth; 7 Beareth all things, believeth all things, hopeth all things, endureth all things, 8 Charity never faileth:…"
(1 Corinthians 13: 4-8).

AS SUCH
2 "Looking unto Jesus the author and finisher of our faith; who for the joy that was set before him endureth the cross, despising the shame, and is set down at the right hand of the throne of God." (Hebrews 12:2)

Now, let's brain storm for a minute

I say that our faith is initiated by a thought or thoughts on or before the substance which caused a chain reaction of hopefulness.

With increased levels of maturity, we simply hope until something happens and trust the outcome that the Lord provides.

So, the key to what I'm trying to say is that it does not matter rather my level of faith began with the sheer hope or captivated by the firsthand account of the Lord's power displayed.

I know now that the foundation of my faith is only sustained by the hope of loving the Lord to exclaim true surrenderance to the greater works which astounds the very core of the gospel aligned with the exuberance of God's character to say I love you Lord!

CHAPTER 6: EXAMINE

Once you have become a disciple of Jesus Christ, your life no longer belongs to you; I come to know that it never did. To address this very factor, I am intrigued by King Solomon insightful view of life. As the early years of King Solomon' life, I guess you can say that he had no worries as a man of great wisdom, riches, & pleasure. However, as King Solomon EXAMINED his life, he realized how vain he had become; and his profound discovery of life & eternity can be summed up to comply:

13 "Let us hear the conclusion of the whole matter: Fear God, and keep his commandments: for this is the whole duty of man." (Ecclesiastes 12:13).

Now, how does one really keep the commandments or adhere to sanctification? Personally, I did not even know this was a question for me until I read the first chapter of Job, and the first verse stood out to me as it reads, "There was a man in the land of Uz, whose name was Job; and that man was perfect and upright, and one that **FEARED** God, and **ESCHEWED** evil." Then, it dawn on me, how one can strive to be perfect and upright before the Lord. Of course, we must reverence the Lord through obedience along with a sincere desire to change & turn away from wickedness... In parallel to rapport, our intent is to always take the way out and choose RIGHTEOUSNESS even when it does not {PAN-OUT} this way.

When we seek God & desire Obedience, it is AMAZING because again even in this----the Lord still takes the lead.

CHAPTER 7: ETERNITY

Literally, Eternity is Everlasting.......

So, why take our Salvation for granted? You see lukewarm Christianity is a DEAD end. In that, Jesus said, 21 Not everyone that saith unto me, Lord, Lord, shall enter into the kingdom of heaven; but he that doeth the will of my Father which is in heaven. 22 Many will say to me in that day Lord, Lord, have we not prophesied in thy name? and in thy name have cast out devils? And in thy name done many wonderful works? 23 And then will I profess unto them, I never knew you: depart from me, ye that work iniquity. (Matthew 7:21-23).

That's why we as believers should not cater to the act of willfully sinning that we may not be FORSAKEN.

To be steadfast on our Christian journey, we must keep in mind that our lives do not belong to us; but it belongs to the Lord. In retrospect, as the Body of Christ, we should never get blind-sided in our so call understanding. Remember, the Lord gives **Wisdom & Understanding**; therefore, we should always pray to stay on track. And don't despise correction even when the Holy Spirit is speaking through fellow brethren. Subsequently, the **Word** is our validation.

Now, if you choose not to seek the Lord and triumph in prayer, you can be an unwanted statistic. 14 For many are called, but few are chosen. (Matthew 22:14).

CHAPTER 8: WILLINGNESS

As I had to revamp this chapter which began with the indepthness of 2Timothy 2:21, " If a man therefore purge himself *from these* (lusts/pride/self-righteousness of sin), he shall be a vessel unto honor, sanctified, and meet for the master's use, and prepared unto every good work."

Then, the Lord told me to look beyond that scriptural passage. I understood that yes we should be about every good work; however, the key is the **willingness** to receive eternity of a privilege to adhere to the Lord's calling.

In such, I am delighted to share about the rich young ruler as I understand that there is an irony of this story despite the rich young ruler's decision as to **SAY** we are all given a choice to **'purge'**… **'from these:**

As such, there was a certain ruler, often known as the rich young ruler.

> *The rich young ruler had a choice to take Jesus at his calling. To paraphrase, 16 the rich young ruler wanted to know what he had to do to inherit eternal life... And Jesus said, 17 you know the commandments. In turn, the rich young ruler said, 20 "all these, have I kept from my youth up.: what lack I yet?" Well, Jesus said, it is still*

one thing you still lack: 21 if thou wilt be perfect go sell that thou haste and give to the poor, and thou shalt have treasure in heaven: and come, follow me. 22 But when the young man heard that saying, he went away sorrowful: for he had great possessions. 23 And when Jesus saw that he was very sorrowful, thy Lord said, <u>that a rich man shall hardly enter into the kingdom of heaven.</u> Now, reread this last sentence, what are your thoughts???? (Matthew 19: 16-30).

Personally,

My thoughts are that it was not sinful for the ruler to be rich. However, as Jesus judged the ruler's life, Jesus knew that this certain ruler's heart was endowed in his riches as he was not WILLING to adhere of the very act of the Lord 'calling vamped by the question the ruler posed himself…What must I do…?

So, this caption of his life came to an unnerved concern from willingness of eternity to the danger of idolization.

idolization in regard
to lusts/pride/self-righteousness
'if it cost'
Rationale: State of Being'
'A willingness of becoming a vessel of honor'

CHAPTER 9: SIN-NATURE

The sin-nature of mankind defies the Lord's will.

In the beginning of creation, this is very much evident. As Adam and Eve were in the Garden of Eden, the Lord God commanded them not to eat "of the tree of the knowledge of good and evil for in the day that thou eatest thereof thou shalt surely die." (Genesis 2:17).

Reflection:

1) Now the serpent was more subtil than any beast of the field which the Lord God had made. And he said unto the woman, Yea, hath God said, Ye shall not eat of every tree of the garden?
2) And the woman said unto the serpent, We may eat of the fruit of the trees of the garden:
3) But of the fruit of the tree which is in the midst of the garden, God hath said, Ye shall not eat of it, neither shall ye touch it, lest ye die.
4) And the serpent said unto the woman, Ye shall not surely die:
5) For God doth know that in the day ye eat thereof, then your eyes shall be opened, and ye shall be as gods, knowing good and evil.
6) And when the woman saw that the tree was good for food, and that it was pleasant to the eyes, and a tree to be desired to make one wise, she took of the fruit thereof, and did eat and gave also unto her husband with her; and he did eat. (Genesis 3: 1-6).

As we know, Eve took the bait as such Adam thereafter which initiated the scheme of satan.

This plot of satan continues to plague mankind as the ultimate demise of the sin-nature is conceptualized through {Pride}. **(I, ME, SELF).**

Therefore, if we do not deny the sin-nature that tries to take charge within us, we can become our own worst enemy of a constant tug-a-war through battle.

Now, let's look further how the sin-nature of Adam and Eve even trickled down even to their offspring as Cain also defied the voice of God.

Of Genesis 4:7, "If thou doest well, shalt thou not be accepted? And if thou doest not well, sin lieth at the door. And unto thee shall be his desire, and thou shalt rule over him." This question and insight was given to Cain to overcome his fallen countenance. But Cain did not adhere to the foretelling of the Lord. And Abel was killed at the hands of his brother <u>Cain</u>. Oh, if _____ would have listened.

Just a reminder, Body of Christ, we are in a battle. But the Lord has given us a way out. We must do RIGHT which the scripture abase to "doest well." In light of it all, we must combat and choose to overcome a fallen countenance of mixed emotions.

Also, the act and temptation of sin is spiritual as the scripture also abase to "sin lieth"; "his desire"; and "over him." Overall, I understand that sin cannot rule over us unless we allow it. In that, the sin-nature is enacted when we cater to the wiles of satan, who became the embodiment of sin along with a third of the angels.

But the good news is that Jesus' **Life & Resurrection** allows us to denounce the temptations that lead to sin; especially, to know that we are REDEEMED.

CHAPTER 10: SEEDETH

THE SEED ≈ MANKIND

Are we going to be the seed that fall on good ground?

OR

Are we going to be that shaky-seed/unpredictable?

The perspective-notion of **SEEDETH** declares witness to stand and live as a child of God or rather to be a yo-yo for satan.

One of my favorite parables told by Jesus Christ is the *sower-of-the-seeds* which transcends a since of **self-examination:**

> 3) And he spake many things unto them in parables, saying, Behold a sower went forth to sow;
>
> 4) And when he sowed, some seeds fell by the wayside, and the fowls came and devoured them up:
>
> 5) Some fell upon stony places, where they had not much earth: and forthwith they sprung up, because they had no deepness of earth:
>
> 6) And when the sun was up, they were scorched; and because they had no root, they withered away.
>
> 7) And some fell among thorns; and the thorns sprung up, and choked them:

8) But other fell into good ground, and brought forth fruit, some an hundredfold, sixtyfold, some thirtyfold. (Matthew 13: 3-8).

***Jesus explains the parable as thus*:**

18) Hear ye therefore the parable of the sower,

19) When any one heareth the word of the kingdom, and understandeth it not, then cometh the wicked one, and catcheth away that which was sown in his heart. This is he which received seed by the wayside.

20) But he that received the seed into stony places, the same is he that heareth the word, and anon with joy receiveth it;

21) Yet hath he not root in himself, but dureth for a while: for when tribulation or persecution ariseth because of the word, by and by he is offended.

22) He also that received seed among the thorns is he that heareth the word; and the care of this world, and the deceitfulness of riches, choke the word, and he becometh unfruitful.

23) But he that received seed into the good ground is he that heareth the word, and understandeth it; which also beareth fruit, and bringeth forth some an hundredfold, some sixty, some thirty. (Matthew 13: 18-23).

SELF-EXAMINATION

By self-examination, I have been that shaky-seed. Due to lack of understanding, I did enact that seed which fall along the wayside. And that seed in stony places as distracted by trials & tribulations with mixed emotions, I thought-Why Lord? Then, to some degree, I had been that seed that fall amongst thorns in which I noticed that I was more complacent when I had plenty which enhanced unpredictability.

With the questions above, there is only (1) answer to be seedeth in the Lord is to trust that he will help us overcome to remain of a stature on good ground.

CHAPTER 11: INTROSPECTION

THE DRAWING=THECALL///&TEMPTATION(S)

Let us not take the drawing of the Lord for granted and the unique experience of **THE CALL**-----rather you were at the altar in the church; in your car; in your bathroom; outside in the yard; in your bedroom; at the hospital; on your job; or in the living room: _____. {YOU FILL IN THE BLANK}

Covertly-we, as believers, did make a commitment to the Lord through repentance as we acknowledged that we were sinners and asked for forgiveness with confession with our mouth that Jesus is the Son of God.

My goodness, it is even clear that Jesus is and has always been which leads me to the third temptation when Jesus came out of the wilderness which represents the **PINNACLE** of introspection as the **drawing=the call//&/temptation(s)** to adore the divineness & love of God and to know that the Word is our only defense to this life race as temptations are inevitable.

THIRD TEMPTION'

5 Then the devil taketh him up into the holy city, and setteth him on a pinnacle of the temple, 6 And saith unto him, If thou be the Son of God, cast thyself down; for it is written, He shall give his angels charge concerning thee: and in their hands they shall bear thee up, lest at any time thou dash thy foot against a stone. 7 Jesus said unto him, It

is written again, Thou shalt not tempt the Lord thy God. (Matthew 4: 5-7).

When I read this particularly about the *'third temptation'*, the Holy Spirit said read it again and again. Then, I begin to pin-point what the devil said, "He shall give his angels charge concerning thee: and in their hands they shall bear thee up, lest at any time thou dash they foot against a stone" With profound revelation, I understood that Jesus left heaven, HIS THRONE, for appointed time for you and me. As SUCH, the devil gave a vivid account of the Lord's divinity.

The nature of the <u>Lord's DIVINENESS</u>,
HALLELUJAH!!!!

This very passage of temptation above brought tears to my eyes to validate how much the Lord loves us.

Of infallibility, Jesus sacrificed his throne for an opportune moment. ------***'begotten of the Father wrapped himself in flesh, born of a virgin, and willingness to substantiate his power & authority by the Lord God's will.'***

Then, there was the first temptation, which relates to the same tactic of satan as it relates to the lust of the flesh: 3 "… If thou be the Son of God command that these stones be made bread. 4 But he answered and said, "It is written, Man shall not live by bread alone, but by every word that proceedth out of the mouth of God." (Matthew 4: 3-4).

Of the third temptation as it alludes to the pride of life 8 "Again the devil taketh him up into an exceedingly high mountain, and sheweth him all the kingdoms of the world, and the glory of them; 9 And saith unto him, All these things will I give thee, if thou wilt fall down and worship me. 10 Then saith Jesus unto him, Get thee hence, satan: for it is written, Thou shalt worship the Lord thy God and him only shalt thou serve." (Matthew 4: 8-10).

We, as the Body of Christ, must be introspective to remember ***the drawing, the call***, ***and be mindful of temptations***' to be victorious of the Lord's divineness.

But keep in mind that satan will always be deceptive with the same temptations of introspection as disguised by the lust of the eyes, the lust of the flesh, and the pride of life which I know all to well.

CHAPTER 12: SELF-PITY

According to The American Heritage dictionary, self-pity means: Exaggerated pity for oneself.

Oh-woe unto I: as self-pity almost got the best of me because I was somehow trapped in the deception that my tears would allow me to excuse myself to be out of the will of the Lord, which triggered a continuous cycle of shallow repentance in doing the same thing over & over again, which my dilemma was always related to truthfulness versus deceit.

Although I desired to do the will of God, the burden of self-pity and unwanted deceit did prevent me from having the peace to do God's will of underlining-**DENIAL.**

As I realize more & more-now, sin or evil of any sort cannot dominate our lives as Christians if we want the Holy Spirit to work mightily within us.

Now, please do not get me wrong, I did not intentionally plan to sin against the Lord. I realized that the unraveling issue of self-pity became most evident during my insecure moments, which is related to FEAR.

FEAR?

The issue of fear had magnified in my life because I simply did not truly rationalized how precious I am to the Lord or comparable to the notion of not good enough which lead to roots which to know there is a root to every problem.

WHAT ROOTS?

Well, as I think back to my childhood til' now, I have had my share of roots: as such with someone telling me why you do not look as beautiful as (so and so); distrust and feeling violated which caused me to be on guard around men if you get my drift; and even those heighten embarrassing situations of limited social capacity, which cause me to secretly isolate myself from others. And subsequently, we can all speculate how satan was involved to the point of honesty I do not even remember the core of these roots as my memories are vague on the surface.

So, my pray is that the Lord revealed any subjective memories to ensure that I am delivered from and strongholds.

With all that to say, self-pity does coincide with fear that can produce roots of a path of demonic oppression and the only defense is---**TRUTH.**

CHAPTER 13: TRUE/WORSHIP

{Praise & Worship}

At a women's conference, I was intrigued when I heard an evangelist say that "everybody can praise the Lord, but everybody will not worship the Lord." Further, the evangelist went on to clarify her statement by the word that 'true worshippers shall worship the Father in spirit and in truth.' (John 4:23).

Although I was intrigued by this notion, I really did not comprehend what it really meant. But now, I know on the surface that worship is when we recognize as believers the sovereignty of the Lord, which exclaims "Who God is!" that God is the reason for our existence and we have a responsibility to live **holy**. As such, I think of praise as an introduction to esteem the goodness of the Lord as worship is ecstatic homage unto Him. As a believer, I praise God to embrace that God is good and not only that HE is perfect!

However, the question that I still have is:
What is true worship?
Going beyond myself
Remembrance
that the Holy Spirit had already given me this answer on numerous occasions'

Now, to expound more on one account, my husband and I were invited to attend the last day that dealt with prophetic teachings. And I must say I was not enthusiastic about going to this conference. Why? In that, I was already dismayed to witness a cycle within the church of the selfish ambitions by others or vice versa the stain of self-righteousness even within myself. Nevertheless, I went anyhow. At most, within the service, I was faced with uncertainty of why I could not press passed **ME…** Therefore, in the…..

Midst

Of

Praise

And

Worship….

{MIDSTY…}

I bowed my head and closed my eyes and prayed; Lord I must decrease…

Still me…

I opened my eyes and tried to sing along…

Still me…

The usher passed out banners to the congregation to wave as I enjoyed waving the silver banner…

Still me…

I closed my eyes again and prayed….

Still me…

I open my eyes again to adhere to the instructions of the Pastor to rally the congregation…Hallelujah!…

Still me…
I looked around the congregation … some in tears…some on bend it knee

some shouting….

Still me…

Then, I bowed my head again and prayed….with sincere Repentance

…. to overcome myself……

Now, as I stood waving the silver banner…..

I felt a sense of comfort to know…

It was not just me, anymore….

With the uplifting of the Holy Spirit…
The Lord's presence….

My tone of voice heightened as I exclaimed, Hallelujah!……….

{Now, my focus is only on the Lord}

I even felt chills over my body……. which sparked…… an unwanted thought…

Are these chills due to the fact that………

the atmosphere was cool in the church?
Maybe'Anyhow

distraction=satan=tempter

Yet,

I thought at the very core of my worship and praise to say,

I Am a Believer in Jesus Christ, and that Settles it!

So, to conclude, true worship and praise extends___ when we forget about……ourselves to surrender all, the only remedy that keeps us is to know that the Lord is GOOD.

There is a day coming'

CHAPTER 14: BELIEVERS

According to the American Heritage dictionary, believe means to accept as true or real, to credit with veracity: I believe you, to have confidence (in); trust: I believe you…; to suppose; think, to have firm faith; believer.

The state of our Salvation is that we believe that Jesus Christ is the Son of God. In that, this is a powerful statement in itself. However, as believers how can this statement mean so much to us; but, so little to others?

Peter delighted me when he said…34 "Of a truth I perceive that God is no respecter of person: 35 But in every nation he that feareth him, and worketh righteousness, is accepted with him. (Acts 10: 34-35).

Despite a person's choice to believe or not, it does not change the fact that the Lord loves us. And the undeniable reason that sets believers apart from others is given by Jesus 23 …If a man loves me, he will keep my words: and my Father will love him, and we will come unto him, and make our abode with him. 24 He that loveth me not keepeth not my sayings: and the word which ye hear is not mine, but the Father's which sent me. (John 14: 23-24).

Presently, the facet of our belief is to accept Jesus Christ which defines us as Christians to profoundly concur even more by the Ethiopian eunuch and Philip:

> 26) And the angel of the Lord spake unto Philip, saying, Arise and go toward the south unto the way that goeth down from Jerusalem unto Gaza, which is desert.

27) And he arose and went: and, behold, a man of Ethiopia, an eunuch of great authority under Candace queen of the Ethiopians, who had the charge of all her treasure, and had come to Jerusalem for to worship.
28) Was returning and sitting in his chariot reading Esaias the prophet?
29) Then the Spirit said unto Philip, Go near, and join thyself to this chariot.
30) And Philip ran thither to him, and heard him read the prophet Esaias, and said, Understandest thou what thou readest?
31) And he said, How can I, except some man should guide me? And he desired Philip that he would come up and sit with him.
32) The place of the scripture which he read was this, He was led as a sheep to the slaughter; and like a lamb dumb before his shearer, so opened he not his mouth:
33) In his humiliation his judgment was taken away; and who shall declare his generation? For his life is taken from the earth.
34) And the eunuch answered Philip, and said, I pray thee of whom speaketh the prophet this? Of himself, or of some other man?
35) Then Philip opened his mouth and began at the same scripture, and preached unto him Jesus.
36) And as they went on their way, they came unto certain water: and the eunuch said, See, here is water; what doth hinder me to be baptized?

37) And Philip said, If thou believest with all thine heart, thou mayest. And he answered and said, I believe that Jesus Christ is the Son of God.
38) And he commanded the chariot to stand still, and they went down both into the water, both Philip and the eunuch; and he baptized him.
39) And when they were come up out of the water, the Spirit of the Lord caught away Philip; that the eunuch saw him no more: and he went on his way rejoicing (Acts 8: 26-39).

Above all else, I must consistently remind myself to rejoice in the fact that our relationship with the Lord is strengthen by our desire to believe IN TRUTH.

CHAPTER 15: FEARLESS

To be fearless as the Body of Christ, we must first fear the Lord. Of Proverbs 9:10, "The fear of the Lord is the beginning of wisdom: and the knowledge of the Holy One is understanding.

Although we are supposed to be fearless in the Body of Christ, again I must admit I have had some serious moments of when fear seemed to be beyond me.

As a very dear friend of mine said how can we have a **mountain top experience** and still have moments in which we as children of God fear.

You know those mountain top experiences were the Lord did something miraculous in your life and we are witnesses of the power and authority in Jesus' name by the Holy Spirit, 17 ... the Spirit of truth; whom the world cannot receive, because it seeth him not, neither knoweth him: but ye know him; for he dwelleth with you, and shall be in you" (John 14:17).

So, the question still remains what brings about fear in the children of God? As I looked back over the fearful moments in my Life, the most common problem is that I was leaning to my own understanding. Therefore, no matter what we think we know, wisdom and understanding only comes from the Lord. And we must take him at his Word.

Always keeping in mind what God has to say------ Jesus said 13 I am Alpha and Omega, the beginning and the end, the first and the last. (Revelation 22:13).

Now, as the Lord commands us to fear Him; the Lord also commands us to fear not.
What's the difference?

First of all, fear is an emotion. In that being said, we know the Lord is not moved or operate on our emotions. To understand the very nature of the Lord, I understand that fear can be holy or unholy. -------- Anything outside of the Lord is unholy.

Therefore, the Spirit of fear can be dominant when we are not in the Lord's will and even when we are subdued by a spiritual attack.

But to fear the Lord is a Holy fear----- Lord God says 11 "For I know the thoughts that I think toward you saith the Lord, thoughts of peace, and not of evil, to give you and expected end." (Jeremiah 29:11).

So, we as the Body of Christ are fearless when we embrace the love of God that only can fully be received through Godly fear to **reverence** the Lord.

According to the American Heritage Dictionary,
REVERENCE means
Profound
Awe
And
Respect...

CHAPTER 16: FERVENTLY

Have you ever thought with a medley in your soul?

It is not bout me, Lord

It is not bout me,

It is not bout me, Lord

It is not bout me"....

Fervently, to my fellow brethren, we must acknowledge that the stability of our Christian journey, 'is not about us'; and especially not built on our feelings or how much more we want the Lord to bless us, but earnestly just **loving the Lord**. In that, I am astonished by Jesus and Peter's conversation.

"LOVEST THOU ME":

15 Simon Peter..., Simon, son of Jonas, lovest thou me more than these? He saith unto him, Yea Lord; thou knowest that I love thee. He saith unto him, Feed my sheep.

16 He saith to him again the second time, Simon, son of Jonas, lovest thou me? He saith unto him, Yea, Lord; thou knowest that I love thee. He saith unto him, Feed my lambs.

17 He saith unto him the third time, Simon, son of Jonas, lovest thou me? Peter was grieved because he said unto him the third time, Lovest thou me? And he said unto him, Lord, thou knowest all things; thou knowest that I love thee. Jesus saith unto him, Feed my sheep. (John 21:15-17)

Oh, can't we see?

I now marvel at the concept of what Jesus Christ meant when He said 'lovest thou me, feed my sheep' as the nature of the third encounter and moment after His crucifixion & resurrection with Peter as even to foretell His great sacrifice unto us all.

And to such a one, Peter had been restored as a true disciple unto the Lord as to uphold the Lord's sweetest purpose that others may come into the **fold.**

Therefore, when I say 'It is not about me', as contrary I am thankful to the Lord that he has saved me unto himself to know that even I and we, as the Body of Christ, have been set to feed thy sheep.

CHAPTER 17: GRACE

'Beyond the knowing to repent'

The simplicity and complexity of words as a whole does shift to the enrichment of the Lord's grace which is heightened more by our personal devotion to the Lord.

Therefore, I understand---**Grace** as the unconditional love of God in action, which is undeniable from Christ's Crucified & Resurrected as the unmerited favor of God, ALREADY FORGIVEN, which is adjacent to God's mercy to escape the pitfall of death by **sanctification** through Jesus Christ.

As such, Grace has so many facets but for the sake of this chapter I would like to focus on (1) criteria as inspired by the Holy Spirit, *'beyond the knowing to repent.'*

One day while I was praying, I had a surreal moment as the Holy Spirit lead me to repent in such a way, tears streamed down my face, and this is when I realized, even more profoundly, that the Lord loved me so much that he <u>*did not want me to*</u> <u>*stay in my sin*</u>.

As further clarification to explain *'beyond the knowing to repent,' is when I, we, as the Body of Christ, liken to the convictions by the Holy Spirit which encompasses our unperishable desire to turn away from sin with the genuine desire to walk uprightly before the Lord.*

So, brethren, inclusively we must realize what the grace of God means to us in such a way that *'beyond the knowing to repent'* inhabits us to cherish **sanctification** through Jesus Christ as true change prevails, **glory to glory.**

CHAPTER 18: CHANGE

So, as I come to the reciprocal of truth that, *how to know that you know that you are saved, ---**Body of Christ*** in such I am given one word by the Holy Spirit, and that is CHANGE. And with this one word, the instruction of Jesus is given, "You have been LUKEWARM long enough;" "Repent, and walk in Obedience."

AND THIS IS A GLIMPSE OF MY LIFE'S STORY THAT LED TO THIS VERY INCLINATION:
Personally,

I thought that the Lord saved me when I repented of my sins as I walked to the altar at my *hom*e church. Thereafter, quote on quote as a 'good' Christian should, I vowed to read my bible every day to live for the Lord. And also at that time, I wrote in my journal and gave an overview of what I read in the bible along with insightful personal revelations.

Of course, I was strengthened for a while as I consistently read the bible. However, my reading of the bible begin to dwindle as my personal journal entries revealed a constant theme, "still something is missing" because I was baffled about the fact that I still had challenges related to sin because even when I repented, I still felt guilty.

(GUILTY)

To reassure myself to overcome this guilt, I always cried out to the Lord and prayed for strength to change which only alluded me as I became complacent in my understanding of church's influence that the Lord loved me no matter what, and surely to know that I was not so bad after all. Also, I was blinded by a superficial view of happiness which was mainly driven by my accomplishments.

*(*ACCOMPLISHMENTS*)*

The accomplishment of being a college graduate with the obtainment of a prestigious job to support my family and all the while being the single mother of two handsome sons as toppled by tremendous support from my precious mom. And there (2006) at *{*G.F.*}* Church, I got married with the blessed addition of two lovely stepdaughters.

To inquire, I looked at my life at its best of correspondence as part of a church organization, dynamics of the family, & career basis.

'DAY TO DAY'

And the correspondence that stood out the most, you guess it, church organization because I always desired to be pleasing to the Lord as I saw church as the framework of life.

But one day, I became more inquisitive when my husband gave his unique testimony of being born again. And with a blink of caliber, my thoughts went from the dynamics of church to saying, **Nothing but Jesus.**

WHAT?

Clueless, this made me contemplate rather are not I was born again. But this notion was short-lived as I stood again on the church's influence of that I know the Lord loved me no matter what, and surely to know that I was not so bad after all.

Nevertheless, time went on as I thought that 'born again' meant striving to be good and when and if I sinned, I just prayed and cried as usually, Lord forgive me.

WELL,

As I continued to be driven by day to day life, I still knew "something is **STILL** missing."

'TWO YEARS PASSED'

In the year of (2008), both my husband and I were seeking God for answers in such I sought the Lord for a closer relationship where I could truly hear his voice. And my husband sought the Lord, as he wanted to know "what must I do Lord?" for specific instructions.

Well, my husband got an answer. With obscurity to contain, my husband was led to the {LDS} church and still to this day we both believe that this phase of our lives was of the Lord's purpose.

Remarkable, during that time, I was baptized by my husband and this was very special to me because I was fully immersed in water as it relates to the bible.

In my youth, I vaguely remember how old I was when I got baptized; I was sprinkled.

OK, OK

When we left the {LDS} church we began to have church at home. However, home teachings were not a new thing for us because we did this early on when we decided to leave {G.F.} Church.

We primarily left *{G.F.}* church due limited travel expenses which hindered us from attending church on a regular basis. As such, we did not want the church to extend more than they had to. Also, to keep in mind my husband and I did give our tithes and offering. So, we just wanted to depend on the Lord for our provision to be at church.

Uh-HUH,

Then, the Lord led us to a non-denominational church *{G.H.}* Ministries in (2009), as the Pastor exclaimed the facet of being born again by the Holy Spirit with accompanying signs of healing and deliverance. I was ecstatic because this validated our home teachings.

Oh, my faith was so strong during this time because I dedicated myself to pray (worship/praise), reading the bible, and even fasting. I would say that this was a good time for me as I saw the awesome power of God not only in my life but others as well.

Eventually, we also decided to leave *{G.H.}* Ministries because we were faced with the same problem as limited finances to travel as such we paid our tithes and offering there faithfully, too.

"WELL THE YEARS PASSED"

Unfortunately, in (2013) as to denote my career, I found myself in a runt because no matter how hard I tried to work I was under constant pressure by satan to compromise and to give into the norm of success to make it anyhow I could.

And let me tell you that this pressure was so dreadful that I was blinded because satan told me the same lie in a different way to which abated me to be drenched in the act of compromise, and I alluded myself to believe the lie.

GOOD AND BAD DAYS

To ease some of my pain, I met a lady that told me about a local church in the community, *{V.C.C}* church, and I thought surely I would feel better if I assembled together with another church assembly. In (2014), my family and I started attending *{V.C.C.}* as I felt a sense of belongingness'.

As I got back into the routine of regular church, I felt more secure in myself especially in my career because I was strengthen for the most part to work hard and to not waiver of any sort.

BUT

As the wave of worldly expectations came crashing in, I said surely a little compromise want hurt besides others were faced with this same challenge and they seemed to be getting along just fine.

OTHERWISE

Of April (2015), which marked the beginning of my overwhelming 4 to 9 month trial, the Holy Spirit said everything was not fine. I know now that I was under strong conviction to **CHANGE** and do what is pleasing to the Lord. And because I still was dull of hearing, I could not abate the chastisement of the Lord.

DISTRESS VS. DOUBT

To cope with my distress or doubt, I even discussed with my present pastor rather are not I needed to leave my job because I became even more consumed by pressures on my job and my lowliness even afforded me to know that work tasks became obscured by demonic activity.

BEFORE ANY RASH DECISION:

My pastor told me to sincerely pray about my situation and as the pastor's wife and my husband gave their input, I was told to do what is pleasing to the Lord.

Well, I did pray but at this time in my life my prayers became few and in-between as there was still no avail because I alluded myself to still think that a little compromise want hurt.

NO RELIEF

Everything was crashing down all around me---- dread, loneliness, confusion, fog memory, anxious-shaky, **EMBARRASSED**, loss of words, insecurity, pure sadness(no laughter or smiles), literally depressed and bitter.

Despite my weakness in which now I call 'shallow repentance', which caused me to override my internal question as such *{still something is missing}*, the hard nature of my FRUSTRATION is that I thought I had already reach a place in God in which I felt, **'*SAFE,*'** to explain concisely I **DID** know what the unconditional love of God felt like.

SO, WHY ME?

And through my reflection, I was shaken by insecurity even more. Then, I realized that I had always dealt with insecurity but I had always been functional in this dysfunction; especially the mindset that the Lord would always come through for me.

Consequently, in this trial, I had no relief even with family & friends' prayers still no change. I felt abandoned by the Lord.

This dread and anxiety got worse to the point I could no longer hide my brokenness, and this turmoil surrounded my career in such a way I had to go ahead and make a decision.

UNCERTAIN

With uncertainty, I left my job of 12.25 years and approximately 10 of those years, I worked as a counselor.

(FLASHBACK)
SYNOSIS

2 months beforehand, I even went to my supervisor to paraphrase, and I told her I do not know what is going on because I cannot keep up with the work demands. As such, I told my supervisor that it probably would be best that 'I **LET** this job go.'

But within my conscious thought, this is what I was really saying to my supervisor, I cannot shake this--- (dread of conviction as uneasiness of feeling the pressure to compromise), should 'I let this job go.'

CALMNESS

Then, my supervisor said Shirley, I am sorry that you feel this way as she went on to say just take-the-time and pray about it. And I did pray; however, I still could not hear the Lord.

OK,

So, one day of that same week in the hallway at work as my supervisor and I, both gradually stopped in the hallway, I told my supervisor, I will just press on, and she gently nodded her head in support of my decision.

WELL,

2 months later the depression became unbearable as I kept giving in to the pressures of work. And it seemed that I was almost taken over by anxiety in my soul, I cried, I cannot go on like this.

SO,

On the most anxious day of my life, I went to my supervisor, and said I have made my decision and I gave her my 30-day notice.

And with a gentle voice, my supervisor said, Shirley, I thought that you already made up your mind. In that brief instant, it made us both chuckle. I went on to say, I am sorry for coming to you again like this------ (unspoken words as such). Then, my supervisor said, "Shirley, life is too short not to be happy and she embraced me with a hug.

30-DAY NOTICE STARTS

I started my 30-day notice, and I still questioned rather or not I made the right decision because the depression and anxiety had gotten **MUCH'** worse. But I managed to carry on until my last day of work.

And I was given a little hope by the wonderful farewell card that my co-workers gave me, I was amazed by their beautiful comments which asseverated my uniqueness because I perceived that they only recognized my vulnerability.

Somehow from this small gesture, I begin to think that this trial was beyond my job.

Now, I would like to say that this gesture was significant because I only knew my co-workers at that office site for 2.25 years as beforehand I was under another supervisor and staff for 10 years which I knew that they saw more of my unique personality.

Furthermore, I am so thankful to have known my former co-workers. Also, the people that I had a pleasure to counsel, I would like to say at my best I gave them my all and I also learned from them as well.

NOW WHAT:
FROM (A) JOB TO (NO) JOB

So, now at home, I began to gradually seek the Lord for answers as I mentioned in Chapter 4, I consistently started praying, fasting, reading my bible, and even walking. Then, to my amazement I could hear the Lord as such the Holy Spirit said, Shirley, you must obey the Lord in everything. Peculiarly, I knew that the Lord had been telling me this all along.

HUMMMM?

And sometime after that during my pray time, the Holy Spirit said instantaneous that this is the answer to your **why me** and to correlate **something is missing**:

Shirley, "You are lukewarm." Tearfully, I knew the Lord was right, because I compromised my faith many times by excusing myself to do wrong and satisfying my own heart's desires.
NOW, NOW, NOW,

With all that being said, I get to this concise point as the reciprocal of truth that *how to know, that you know, that you are saved, ---Body of Christ*, we are TRULY saved because you and I decided to **CHANGE**---no longer intrusiveness to sin willfully as the grace of the Lord gives us the strength to live holy. And ecstatically, I can say already forgiven as we stand for righteousness with the conceivable purpose to reach others. *(HOW ABOUT THAT!)*

POEM---'MY, MY'

MY, MY

The Lord did not save me because of the church I attend
'MY, MY'
The Lord did not save me to ensure my life accomplishments of
Church; College; Career; Family;
'MY, MY'
The Lord did not save me to bestow infinite blessings
'MY, MY'
The Lord did not save me just to portray
His awesome power
healings
deliverances
'MY, MY'
However, the state of Salvation is the belief in Jesus,
'MY, MY'
TRUE Repentance, not shallow
'MY, MY'
The water Baptism as a symbol of the outward commitment
OLD ME-----THE NEW ME
'MY, MY'
The Lord did not save me just when I became born again
On, before, or after the water baptism
'MY, MY'
'Just to say,
I am not only saved because of my born again experience

As the perfect alignment
When my soul conformed to my Spirit,
Yes Lord,
Then of an instance the Holy Spirit did come,
Awesome Wonder,
'MY, MY,
I said all of this to say,
CHANGE
HOLINESS IS RIGHT
'MY, MY'
AND BY FAITH
'MY, MY,
TO BE SAVED
MY, MY!
IT'S CHRIST THAT LIVED IN ME
MY, MY!
As eternity awakes us all, I often wonder what the Lord might say:
Shirley, I saved you because you believed in me,
You were water baptized,
Reborn,
Filled with the Holy Spirit
'MY, MY'
Your path of Life was shady and Stoney, at times.
'MY, MY'
You had some weary days
Waring
Against
Good and evil
'MY, MY'

***BUT** my Grace and Mercy is sufficient for thee*
BECAUSE
Liken to my chastising
Shirley,
You woke up to my truths;
Especially to say
It is better to obey the Lord
Rather than Man
&
All ears to hear,
One day
Well done, my good and faithful servant.

"ETERNITY IS EVERLASTING"

I can only concede, to the words inspired by the Lord, Come out of her my people, that ye be not partakers of her sins, and that ye receive not of her plagues, Revelation 18:4.

ENDNOTES:

The KJV Foundation Study Bible: Copyright 2015 by Thomas Nelson.

The American Heritage, dictionary: Dell Book; Fourth Edition; Copyright 2001 by Houghton Mifflin Company) {80};{285};{715};{754}.

www.ingramcontent.com/pod-product-compliance
Lightning Source LLC
Chambersburg PA
CBHW071757040426
42446CB00012B/2604